Sawgrass Poems

a view of the everglades

Poems by FRANK ASCH   Photographs by TED LEVIN

A GULLIVER GREEN BOOK   HARCOURT BRACE & COMPANY   San Diego   New York   London

Text copyright © 1996 by Frank Asch
Introduction and Notes copyright © 1996 by Ted Levin
Photographs copyright © 1996, 1995, 1994, 1988, 1986, 1985 by Ted Levin

Requests for permission to make copies of any part of the work should
be mailed to: Permissions Department, Harcourt Brace & Company,
6277 Sea Harbor Drive, Orlando, Florida 32887-6777.

Gulliver Green is a registered trademark of Harcourt Brace & Company.

Library of Congress Cataloging-in-Publication Data
Asch, Frank.
Sawgrass poems: a view of the Everglades: poems by Frank Asch;
photographs by Ted Levin.—1st ed.
p. cm.
"A Gulliver green book."
Summary: Poems and photographs provide a picture
of the unique ecosystem of the Florida Everglades.
ISBN 0-15-200180-8
1. Children's poetry, American. 2. Everglades (Fla.)—Poetry. [1. Everglades
(Fla.)—Poetry. 2. American poetry.] I. Levin, Ted, ill.
PS3551.S3S28 1996
811'.54—dc20 95-22762

First edition   A B C D E

Printed in Singapore

The author and photographer would like
to thank the following people for their help in making this book:
Rob Bennetts, Mike and Sue Wilson, Peter Allen, and Isobel Kalafarski.

FRONT and BACK COVER PHOTO: Sawgrass.
Everglades National Park, Florida, July 1993.
TITLE PAGE PHOTO: Snail kite with apple snail.
Littoral zone of Lake Okeechobee, Florida, April 1994.
DEDICATION PAGE PHOTO: Halloween pennant dragonfly on a
seedhead of sawgrass. Everglades National Park, Florida, July 1993.
COLOPHON PAGE PHOTO: Tree snail in a hardwood hammock
in a pinelands. Everglades National Park, Florida, March 1993.

To birdman Rob Bennetts
——F. A.

*To Casey, with love——may his Everglades be wet
and full of birds*
——T. L.

Introduction

The Everglades is a wetland wilderness, born in the sky and sustained by rain. It has no winter, summer, fall, or spring, like the rest of North America. Instead, like the tropics, the Everglades has two seasons—wet and dry. During the dry season, from November to April, the seemingly endless stretches of grassy marshes are brown and brittle, and the sky is blue, horizon to horizon. During the wet season, from May to October, the landscape is green and lush and looks like a wide, shallow, slow-moving river.

Five thousand years ago, Ice Age sea levels began to recede and the Everglades developed on a plain of limestone, which tilts down less than two inches per mile from Lake Okeechobee to Florida Bay. Over many hundreds of years, *hammocks*, which are bumps above the water level in the limestone, became seeded by tropical trees. Holes in the limestone filled with muck and attracted water-loving cypress trees to form *domes*. Shallow grooves in the limestone, called *sloughs* (pronounced *slews*), spotted with water lilies and insect-eating bladderworts, became the main channels of the Everglades. Just about everything else is now covered with sawgrass—which is not a grass at all, but a spiky-edged sedge. There are miles and miles of sawgrass, which grows dense or sparse, tall or short.

Nowhere else in North America do plants and animals of both the temperate zone and the tropics mingle. Nowhere else in America can you see manatees and crocodiles; or one-hundred-foot-tall royal palms; or bouquets of orchids and colorful snails festooning trees like Christmas decorations. In the Everglades, panthers and black bears weave trails through the sawgrass; rabbits swim between the hammocks, trying to escape hungry bobcats and gray foxes; grasshoppers grow four inches long and become so fat that they cannot fly; freshwater turtles, as big as kitchen sinks, break the surface with their periscope noses. In the dry season, as pools of water begin to shrink, engineering alligators dig holes to stay wet, and water-loving animals—otters, fish, snakes, frogs, turtles, snails, crayfish—join them. Thousands of herons, egrets, ibis, and storks feast on the trapped fish, cover the crowns of mangroves like fresh snow, and decorate the Florida skies in one of America's wild and wondrous pageants. The vitality of spawning fish and insects, the determination of spiders that rebuild their webs each day, the songs of frogs in the star-studded night transform the Everglades from wetland to wonderland, a source of earthly inspiration.

In 1947, Harry S. Truman dedicated the tip of south Florida as Everglades National Park. It was the first national park in the world to be preserved for its unusual gathering of plants and animals rather than its spectacular geologic scenery. Now, almost fifty years later, the Everglades has another unique distinction. It is the only national park threatened with extinction.

Water is the very soul of the Everglades, but nearby man-made dikes and levees interrupt its flow. Canals drain water away from the sloughs and send it to the ocean. When water finally reaches the Everglades National Park, it often arrives at the wrong time of year, polluted by runoff from the farm fields. Sometimes the park gets too much water. Sometimes it gets too little. Now, teams of biologists, hydrologists, engineers, and politicians have pledged to help restore the flow of water by removing some of the levees, plugging some of the canals, and cleaning the farmland runoff. No one knows if the Everglades, which has survived for over five thousand years, will survive for fifty more.

These poems and photographs are a celebration of the Everglades. Frank and I want her to speak for herself. If, after sitting with this book, you want to immerse yourself in the southern tip of Florida, we have succeeded. Long may she flow and her wild winds blow.

—TED LEVIN
Thetford, Vermont

In the Glare

The glare of sunrise
deceives my eyes.
Heat waves ripple.
Tropical birds fill my ears
with exotic cries.
Expectations triple.
Am I in a jungle?
Panthers roam here.
Or in the Amazon?
Gators feel at home here.
Am I in a desert
where it's hot and dry?
Well, the Glades
are hot all right.
But they're not dry!
And the only zebra
I can see
is the zebra
butterfly.

Two Baby Snail Kites

Two baby snail kites
sitting in their nest,
hungry and endangered,
hoping for the best.

Apple snails for dinner.
Apple snails for lunch.
And every Sunday morning,
apple snails for brunch.

Two baby snail kites,
eyes still and steady,
waiting for a meal,
mouths wide and ready!

Apple snails for dinner.
Apple snails for lunch.
And every Sunday morning,
apple snails for brunch.

"Hey Mom! Hey Dad!
How about some meat?"
"So sorry, little ones.
Snails is what we eat."

Apple snails for dinner.
Apple snails for lunch.
And every Sunday morning,
apple snails for brunch.

Alligator Hotel

When skies are dry and temperatures cool
alligators dig hotels in the muck,
and frogs and birds and snakes and turtles
check in for the winter months.
Soon the egrets and herons arrive,
and bass and gar and bream
unpack their bags and go for a swim.
Greeting his patrons with a smile,
the gracious gator basks in the sun.
He dreams of dinosaur days
and Jurassic nights,
of hoisting a sail upon his back
and escaping from hunters' guns
and Miccosukee Indians
who want to wrestle him.
He dreams of a wind
that could carry him far away
from alligator bags and alligator shoes,
far away from all his alligator blues.
He dreams and he rests
and, when he feels that certain emptiness
in his belly, he slips into the water
and eats one of his guests.

Hey You, Manatee!

You're no mermaid mama.
Yes, that's true!
But I can understand
how those ancient sailors
fell in love with you.
You whisker-nosed blubber blob!
You seaweed-munching sea slob!
You mossbacked moat goat,
slow-motion victim of speedboat!
Quietly munching
cow of the sea,
I confess—
I love you, manatee!

If I Had a Vulture

I want to get a pet
to have and to hold.
Not a pretty pet,
but one that's black and bold.
Dogs are always sleeping.
Cats don't care.
I don't want a guinea pig.
I don't want a hare.
I want to get a pet
not like all the rest.
I wouldn't mind a cobra,
but a vulture would be best!
I've seen them in the Everglades,
waiting in the trees,
cutting circles in the sky,
banking on the breeze.
If I had a vulture,
I'd make sure he ate
all the yucky stuff
from my dinner plate.

If I had a vulture,
it would be so gruesome!
I'd dress myself in black,
so we could be a twosome.
If I had a vulture,
he could come to school,
riding on my shoulder.
We would look so cool!

Some Rivers

Some rivers rush to the sea.
They push and tumble and fall.
But the Everglades is a river
with no hurry in her at all.
Soaking the cypress
that grows so tall;
nursing a frog,
so quiet and small;
she flows but a mile
in the course of a day,
with plenty of time
to think on the way.

But how can she cope
with the acres of corn
and sorrowful cities that drain her?
With hunters and tourists and levees
that chain and stain and pain her?
Does the half of her that's left
think only of the past?
Or does she think of her future
and how long it will last?
Some rivers rush to the sea.
They push and tumble and fall.
But the Everglades is a river
with no hurry in her at all.

Water Moccasin

Curled like a rope
a water moccasin
lies in the sun.

I look at him.
He looks at me.
And I remember a friend
who once attacked a black snake
just to see it
twist
and
writhe
and
squirm.

Curled like a rope
a water moccasin
lies in the sun.

I look at him.
He looks at me.
But who's really in danger?
Who's the lethal one?

In the Beginning

In the beginning, when the earth was new,
birds had no feet but only flew.
When they crashed upon their nose,
Mother Nature gave them toes.
Then they dined standing on the beach,
catching all the fish within their reach.
And when they fought for fish to eat,
Mother Nature stretched their feet.
"Nobody here can fall asleep!
So, you long-legged birds, fish in the deep.
Short-legged birds, fish near the shore.
And stop that fighting! You hear? No more!"

Old Man Mangrove

Old Man Mangrove
lives by the sea.
He's a sailor, he's a farmer,
he's a rookery.

All year long he
drops green leaves,
enriching the soil
for other trees.

Shrimp and lobster
spawn on his farms.
Thousands of birds
nest in his arms.

Covered in oysters,
living on land,
he seems to creep
across the sand.

He moves at the pace
of a tired old snail,
till the tide comes in
and he sets sail.

Those Eyes

I held you in my hands,
    heart

    beat,

    wing

    throb.
And those eyes,
brighter than blood,
deeper than song,
made me believe
if only we could see
through those eyes

    nothing

    on

    this

    planet

    could

    ever

    be

    the

    same.

I Know What
You're Thinking

I know what you're thinking:
"How smooth, how swift, how sleek!"
I know what you're thinking:
"What poise, what grace, how chic!"

You watch me catch a fish
and climb ashore to eat it.
You admire my dexterity
and wish you could repeat it.

I see admiration,
even envy, on your face.
You seek an otter's life—
a chance to take my place.

But there are gators where I swim.
My life is not all play.
Sometimes I am the hunter.
Sometimes I am the prey.

My Little Mosquito

All night you kept me tossing, tangled in my bed,
hiding in my sleeping bag, slapping at my head.
In the morning light you're very plain to see.
With a single blow I could kill you instantly.
But when I see my blood glowing red in you,
I stop to think what I should do.
You did not attack me out of greed;
without my blood, you could not breed.
I will live a long life. You will die quite soon—
in a few days, give or take an afternoon.
And it's nice to know a part of me
will help you raise your family.
So I unzip my tent and let you go—
"Fly to your destiny, my little mosquito!"

The Spider
Is a Lovely Lady

The spider is a lovely lady.
She knows just what to do.
She weaves a dainty web
to catch the morning dew.

The spider is a lovely lady.
She lives among the trees.
Her babies are so small
they float upon the breeze.

They spin a silken thread
that lifts them in the air.
"Take me home," they whisper.
And it brings them there.

The Strangler Fig

It's just a matter of time
until the strangler fig
commits the perfect crime.
Stealthy stalker,
Jack the Gripper,
he wheedles his way
up the victim's trunk,
day after day.
Squeezing ever stronger
week after week,
year after year,
he grows
fatter, thicker, longer!
While you grow accustomed
to his face,
he grows to take
his victim's
place.

Preening

Preening every day,
what a chore!
Wing up,
leg out,
tuck,
twist,
and stretch.

Preening every day,
what a bore!
Wing down,
leg in,
bend,
reach,
and nibble.

Preening every day
is the price we pay
to crouch,
spring,
and soar!
Flying day and night,
what a delight!

Who Cuts the Sawgrass?

Who cuts the sawgrass
and trims it with a blade?
Who sweats until it's done
and rests in the shade?

Fire cuts the sawgrass
and trims it with a blade.
Fire sweats until it's done
and rests in the shade.

Who puts out the fire
and wrestles down the flame?
Who beats it with a stick
until it's cold and tame?

Rain puts out the fire
and wrestles down the flame.
Rain beats it with a stick
until it's cold and tame.

A Panther's Life

I ate the meat
my mother brought me.
I grew big
and strong.

      I learned to stalk
      the way my mother showed me.
      I grew fast
      and smart.

            I learned to live
            the way my mother taught me.
            I roam far
            and

                        alone.

Hurricane Song

You can crack me.
You can smash me.
You can snap me.
You can slash me.

You can knock me down,
but not for very long.
I'll come back again,
tall and green and strong.

You can whip me.
You can drench me.
You can slit me.
You can wrench me.

You can knock me down,
but not for very long.
When you have blown away,
I'll come back
tall and green and strong.

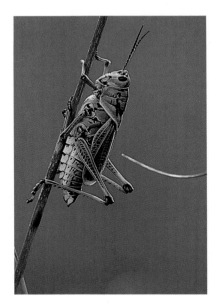

Safe At Last

I took the Everglades
and put it in my car.
I had to squeeze a bit
but home was not too far.

I put gators in the garden,
herons in the hall,
bobcats in the bedroom,
orchids on the wall.

Panthers in the playroom,
spoonbills in the sink,
ibis in the icebox.
What will Mother think?

I put sawgrass in the sunroom
and then I shut the door.
The Everglades is safe now.
I will not worry anymore!

Stillness

Stillness waits
for sun to shine,
for mist to clear,
for tide to shift,
for breeze to blow.
Stillness waits
in the mangrove,
in the sawgrass,
in the slough,
and the soggy
cypress dome.
Stillness waits
for rush of rain,
for snap of jaw,
for splash of seed,
and gator growl.
And still,
stillness waits
for sun to set,
for moon to rise
and stars to shine.

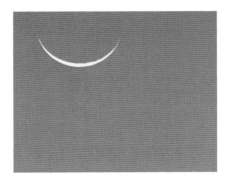

Notes and Photo Captions

In the Glare

In the wet season the Everglades looks like a river; in the dry season it looks like a savanna. Sixty-one percent of the vegetation, and many species of birds and butterflies—like the zebra butterfly—are tropical, most of them originally from the Caribbean. The rest of the species of plants and animals in south Florida are native to the eastern United States.

LEFT PHOTO: Sunrise and mist with silhouetted slash pines in the southern Everglades. *Everglades National Park, Florida, February 1990.* RIGHT PHOTO: Zebra butterfly. *Otter Hammock, Shark Valley, Everglades National Park, Florida, February 1993.*

Two Baby Snail Kites

Snail kites are an endangered tropical member of the hawk clan. In the United States they are found only in the state of Florida between the St. Johns River and the Everglades. Because snail kites feed almost exclusively on apple snails—large freshwater mollusks that rise to the surface of the water to breathe—these kites are particularly vulnerable to the draining and diversion of the Everglades. Anything that affects the well-being of the apple snail dramatically affects the snail kite.

LEFT PHOTO: Adult male snail kite. *Lake Okeechobee, Florida, March 1994.* RIGHT PHOTO: Snail kite chicks viewed from a blind wedged in Everglades muck. *Water Conservation Area 3A, Florida, April 1994.*

Alligator Hotel

Alligators (and crocodiles) belong to the ancient group of reptiles called *archosaurs*. Using their snouts and feet, alligators dig out vegetation and muck that has accumulated in holes in the limestone. During the dry season, "gator holes" hold water and become sanctuaries not only for alligators but also for concentrations of other aquatic creatures. Of course, alligators feed on their "guests." Once hunted to the brink of extinction, alligator populations have recovered in Florida. Miccosukee Indians, who have lived in the Everglades for nearly two hundred years, wrestle alligators on their reservation to entertain tourists.

LEFT PHOTO: Alligator and reflected light. *Mrazek Pond, Everglades National Park, Florida, January 1988.* RIGHT PHOTO: Alligator holding a Florida softshell turtle. *Eco Pond, Everglades National Park, Florida, February 1992.*

Hey You, Manatee!

Manatees are aquatic vegetarians distantly related to elephants. Like whales, these gentle, gregarious mammals give birth in the water. Although manatees have no known predators, they are frequently injured or killed by speeding powerboats that do not see them lounging beneath the surface of the water. Because manatees rise vertically and their paired mammary glands—which are very humanlike—rest on the surface of the water, sailors have, for centuries, mistaken them for mermaids.

LEFT PHOTO: Two manatees nuzzling. *Crystal River, Florida, December 1983.* RIGHT PHOTO: Manatee. *Crystal River, Florida, January 1985.*

If I Had a Vulture

Two species of vultures live in Florida: the black vulture and the turkey vulture. Both species may soar for hours in a search for carrion. Their almost featherless heads are easy to clean and therefore an advantage for feeding on rotting carcasses, but this baldness makes them less than beautiful to human eyes. Vultures idling stiff-winged above the Everglades, however, are a most inspiring sight.

LEFT PHOTO: Adult turkey vulture. *Arizona-Sonora Desert Museum, Tucson, Arizona, April 1990.* RIGHT PHOTO: A flock of turkey vultures at sunset near the mouth of Lostmans River, heading to roost in the standing dead mangroves that were killed by Hurricane Andrew. *Everglades National Park, Florida, January 1994.*

Some Rivers

Marjory Stoneman Douglas, in her book *The Everglades: River of Grass* (1947), called the Everglades a river. Although this metaphor has become synonymous with the region, the Everglades is actually the largest freshwater marsh in North America, one hundred miles long and about fifty miles wide (at its widest). Before the central and northern Everglades were diked and dammed, a high count of nearly 265,000 wading birds nested in the mangroves at the interface of fresh and salt water in Everglades National Park. Now the number of wading birds has fallen to about 18,500.

LEFT PHOTO: Cornfield at the boundary of Everglades National Park. *Florida City, Florida, November 1993.* RIGHT PHOTO: Green tree frog on saw palmetto leaf. *Lake Kissimmee State Park, Florida, December 1989.*

Water Moccasin

Water moccasins are one of four species of poisonous snakes that live in the Everglades. (The other three are the eastern coral snake, pigmy rattlesnake, and eastern diamondback rattlesnake.) Water moccasins feed primarily on fish and frogs. When threatened, they spread their jaws and show the white lining of their mouth, which is why they are also called *cottonmouths*. Like all snake venom, the venom of water moccasins is an enzyme that serves to kill and digest their food. Water moccasins are not aggressive, however, and will not attack unless molested. The threat they pose to humans has been greatly exaggerated.

In the Beginning

When a group of bird species share the same habitat and food resources, they often evolve by adapting physically in order to minimize competition. The varying lengths of the legs of wading birds allow different species of herons, egrets, and ibis to coexist in the same drying pools. Species-specific behavior further reduces competition: black-crowned and yellow-crowned night herons feed after the sun goes down; tiny least bitterns hang on cattail stalks and strike out at fish and dragonflies; green-backed herons feed in the shallows or from a perch; snowy egrets feed in deeper water and while flying; great egrets and great blue herons feed in even deeper water.

Old Man Mangrove

Mangrove forests are found in quiet tidal waters throughout the tropics worldwide. In the Everglades there are three species of mangroves, each with a different tolerance to water depth, time of submersion at high tide, and concentration of salt in the water. Because they continually shed their nutrient-rich leaves, mangrove forests are among the most biologically productive zones in the world. The decomposing fallen leaves form the basis of an elaborate food chain.

Those Eyes

On January 31, 1994, an event happened that inspired this poem. A great blue heron that had gorged on fish and was too heavy to take flight flapped helplessly in Water Conservation Area 3A in the Everglades. Thinking the bird might be suffering from mercury poisoning, my guide, biologist Rob Bennetts, Frank, and I airboated over. I threw my windbreaker over the heron's head to calm it down—and to protect myself from its lethal, daggerlike bill—and brought it onto the boat. Frank held the heron in his lap while we returned to the landing to give the bird to a heron specialist. Under normal circumstances, however, wild birds should not be handled by humans.

I Know What You're Thinking

Otters are the only members of the weasel family in North America whose males stay with the females and help raise the young. These mammals are such efficient hunters of fish and crayfish that they have plenty of time left over for lighthearted play. In years of severe drought, otters are forced into shrinking pools of water, where they often fall prey to alligators.

LEFT PHOTO: River otter on a fallen cypress log. *Roberts Strand, Big Cypress National Preserve, Florida, January 1994.* RIGHT PHOTO: Alligator in a pinelands pond. *Everglades National Park, Florida, February 1985.*

My Little Mosquito

There are forty-three species of mosquitoes in Everglades National Park. Fortunately, only the females suck blood. They require high-protein meals to produce eggs. Male mosquitoes, which look like midges, feed on fruit juices and nectar and inadvertently pollinate many Everglades flowers. Larval mosquitoes, which hang upside down from the surface of the water, are eaten by mosquito fish, which are eaten by bass and gar, which, eventually, are eaten by herons and alligators.

LEFT PHOTO: Mosquito stuck on an insectivorous sundew. *Houghton Lake, Michigan, July 1985.*

The Spider Is a Lovely Lady

Spiders are members of a group of invertebrates called *arachnids*, which are closely related to insects. The golden orb weaver is a tropical spider that probably ballooned to Florida from the Caribbean. Tiny spiderlings climb up vegetation, let out a line of silk, catch the wind, and

set sail; eventually they land, sometimes hundreds of miles away. The yellow web of the golden orb weaver attracts flower-seeking bees, which the spiders wrap with silk and eat.

LEFT PHOTO: Golden orb weaver at the edge of a hardwood hammock in a pinelands. *Everglades National Park, Florida, July 1993.* RIGHT PHOTO: Sheet webs and sawgrass at sunrise. *Off the Flamingo Road, Everglades National Park, Florida, July 1993.*

The Strangler Fig

The seeds of the strangler fig often germinate on the branches of rough-barked trees such as cabbage palms and live oaks. Birds eat the fig's red berries and pass the seeds unharmed. Attaching to the branch of the host tree, the seedling strangler fig sends its roots downward and its leaves and branches upward. After many years the strangler fig grows around its host, often killing it and taking its place in the forest.

LEFT PHOTO: Strangler fig on an old-growth cypress. *Fakahatchee Strand State Preserve, Florida, December 1992.* RIGHT PHOTO: Strangler fig on a ficus tree. *Fakahatchee Strand State Preserve, Florida, March 1993.*

Preening

Birds preen several times a day to realign and clean their feathers. Most species of birds have a uropygial gland, also called an oil gland or a preen gland, just above the base of the tail. Birds smear a secretion of fatty acids and wax from the glands onto their bills, then carefully rub it off on the feathers of their bodies and wings. Without the daily ritual of preening, a bird's feathers would lose their ability to insulate and stay waterproof, and also to govern flight. Flightless terrestrial birds—ostriches, rheas, emus, cassowaries—do not have uropygial glands.

FAR LEFT PHOTO: Great egret. *Anhinga Trail, Everglades National Park, Florida, December 1992.* NEAR LEFT PHOTO: Immature white ibis. *Eco Pond, Everglades National Park, Florida, January 1994.* RIGHT PHOTO: Adult white ibis with immature white ibis. *Eco Pond, Everglades National Park, Florida, January 1994.*

Who Cuts the Sawgrass?

There are more lightning strikes in Florida than in any other state in America. Most lightning-caused wildfires in the Everglades occur at the beginning of the wet season. Some plant communities, such as sawgrass marshes and pinelands, depend on wildfires for survival because repeated burning eliminates fire-sensitive plants that would otherwise transform the plant community. In the sawgrass marshes, fire burns off the previous year's growth and kills encroaching willows. But within a day or two, new green sawgrass shoots appear. In pinelands, fire kills shade-loving tropical hardwood trees that thrive in the shadow of pines. This allows pine seeds, which require more sunlight, to germinate.

LEFT PHOTO: Aerial view of Shark River Slough. *Water Conservation Area 3A, Florida, April 1994.* RIGHT PHOTO: Control burn. *Fakahatchee Strand State Preserve, Florida, March 1994.*

A Panther's Life

The Florida panther is a remnant subspecies of the mountain lion. Although Florida panthers once ranged from Arkansas to Virginia, they are now restricted to extreme southwestern Florida. The panther's favorite foods are white-tailed deer and wild hogs, but panthers also eat raccoons, armadillos, alligators, and occasionally bobcats. From the time they are grown, Florida panthers live solitary lives. Recently the United States Fish and Wildlife Service and the Florida Game and Fresh Water Fish Commission began releasing Texas mountain lions in south Florida to mate with the panthers and bolster their dwindling population.

RIGHT PHOTO: Captive panther outside Big Cypress National Preserve. *Immokalee, Florida, January 1982.*

Hurricane Song

Florida is hit by more hurricanes than any other state in America. As destructive as hurricanes are, the plants and animals of the Everglades are adapted to them. In fact, many plant communities have been shaped by the passage of tropical storms. Wind and waves disperse the cigar-shaped seedlings of red mangroves, which germinate on the parent tree. At the same time, the hurricane topples old trees or buries aerial roots with sediment, which kills the mangroves. A coastal hurricane may stir up the bottom of Florida Bay and set up new patterns of tidal circulation within the bay. The rain from one wet hurricane can make the difference between a "dry" year and a "wet" year. Not all hurricanes are wet, however; powerful Hurricane Andrew, for instance, dropped only two inches of water, while less powerful Hurricane Gordon dropped eight inches.

LEFT *and* RIGHT PHOTOS: Pinelands after the passage of Hurricane Andrew. *Everglades National Park, Florida, September 1992.*

Safe at Last

Much is being done to save the Everglades. The Army Corps of Engineers, the government agency that built the dams and dikes that disrupted the flow of water in the Everglades, has been mandated to restore a more "natural" timing, volume, and distribution to the flow of water in south Florida. The state of Florida has purchased the farmland, called the Frog Pond, from which the headwaters of Taylor Slough originate. Taylor Slough is the largest drainage in the southeastern Everglades and the source of water for the popular Anhinga Trail in Everglades National Park. Biologists are busy uncovering facts about the natural histories of tree snails, apple snails, snail kites, crocodiles, heron rookeries, and seasonal distributions of fish, all of which are critical to understanding the true nature of the Florida Everglades. These findings will help direct the restoration effort. The National Audubon Society has made the restoration of the Everglades one of their prime goals for the 1990s. Together with the Wilderness Society, the Sierra Club, and several other nonprofit organizations, the National Audubon Society has formed the Everglades Coalition, whose goal is to work with government agencies to help with restoration.

LEFT PHOTOS *(clockwise)*: Squirrel tree frog. *Shark Valley, Everglades National Park, Florida, February 1985.* Wild pine flower. *Cypress dome near Pay-hay-okee Overlook, Everglades National Park, Florida, February 1990.* Eastern Lubber grasshopper on sawgrass. *Everglades National Park, Florida, July 1993.* RIGHT PHOTO: Spanish moss on live oak. *Lake Kissimmee State Park, Florida, January 1993.*

Stillness

Even with all its problems, Everglades National Park retains a raw majestic beauty and the timeless character of primordial nature. With restoration under way, the health of the Everglades will surely improve over time.

LEFT PHOTO: Sunrise at Sandy Key. *Florida Bay, Everglades National Park, Florida, December 1993.* RIGHT PHOTO: Canoe moon at sunset over Florida Bay. *Everglades National Park, Florida, February 1991.*

—TED LEVIN

The photographs in this book were taken with Nikon camera bodies

and lenses, ranging from 24mm to 800mm, off a Gitzo tripod.

The film used was Fuji 50 & 100, Fuji Velvia, and Kodachrome 25 & 64.

The display and text type were set in Centaur.

Color separations by Bright Arts, Ltd., Singapore

Printed and bound by Tien Wah Press, Singapore

This book was printed with soya-based inks on Leykam recycled

paper, which contains more than 20 percent postconsumer waste

and has a total recycled content of at least 50 percent.

Production supervision by Warren Wallerstein and Pascha Gerlinger

Designed by Camilla Filancia